Christmas in the United Kingdom

Christmas in the United Kingdom

Christmas Around the World
from World Book

World Book, Inc.
a Scott Fetzer company
Chicago

Staff

Executive Committee

President
Donald D. Keller

Vice President and Editor in Chief
Paul A. Kobasa

Vice President, Sales and Marketing
Sean Lockwood

Vice President, Marketing and Digital Development
Sean Klunder

Vice President, International
Richard Flower

Director, Human Resources
Bev Ecker

Editorial

Associate Director, Supplementary Publications
Scott Thomas

Managing Editor, Supplementary Publications
Barbara A. Mayes

Senior Editor
Kristina Vaicikonis

Researcher
Annie Brodsky

Administrative Assistant
Ethel Matthews

Manager, Contracts & Compliance (Rights & Permissions)
Loranne K. Shields

Graphics and Design

Senior Manager
Tom Evans

Coordinator, Design Development and Production
Brenda B. Tropinski

Senior Designer
Isaiah Sheppard

Manager, Cartographic Services
Wayne K. Pichler

Manufacturing/Production

Director
Carma Fazio

Manufacturing Manager
Barbara Podczerwinski

Production/Technology Manager
Anne Fritzinger

Proofreader
Emilie Schrage

Marketing

Director, Direct Marketing
Mark R. Willy

Marketing Analyst
Zofia Kulik

Editorial Administration

Director, Systems and Projects
Tony Tills

Senior Manager, Publishing Operations
Timothy Falk

Associate Manager, Publishing Operations
Audrey Casey

Library of Congress Cataloging-in-Publication Data
Christmas in the United Kingdom.
    p. cm. -- (Christmas around the world)
    Summary: "Customs and traditions of the Christmas holidays as celebrated in England, Scotland, and Wales. Includes crafts, recipes, and carols"--Provided by publisher.
    ISBN 978-0-7166-0822-6
    1. Christmas--Great Britain. 2. Great Britain--Social life and customs. 3. Christmas around the world from World Book.
    I. World Book, Inc.
    GT4987.43.C49 2012
    394.2663--dc23
                    2012020275

World Book, Inc.
233 N. Michigan Ave.
Chicago, Illinois 60601

Printed in China by Shenzhen Donnelley Printing Co., Ltd., Guangdong Province
1st printing September 2012

The editors gratefully acknowledge the cooperation of the British Tourist Authority.
Carols from THE INTERNATIONAL BOOK OF CHRISTMAS CAROLS, copyright © 1963, 1980 by Walter Ehret and George K. Evans. © Walton Music Corp. Used by permission.

The village of Castle Combe in Wiltshire, in southwestern England, lies beneath a dusting of snow in the days before Christmas. ▶

Contents

Sights and Sounds of Yuletide London

Four great bronze lions guard Trafalgar Square in the center of London. High above, on a towering granite column, looms the famous statue of Lord Nelson, the British admiral who defeated the combined French and Spanish fleets at Trafalgar in Britain's greatest naval victory. A pair of splendid fountains fill the early evening air with mist. And between them stands a magnificent Christmas tree, topped by a glowing white star.

Lights twinkle on the tree as the chilly breeze stirs its dark green branches. Except for the lights, it looks as if it might still be growing in the cold Norwegian forest from which it came. The giant spruce is a gift from Norway. Each year since 1947, the city of Oslo has sent a tree to the city of London, in gratitude for the help of the British people to Norway while the country was occupied by Nazi Germany during World War II (1939–1945).

In the weeks before Christmas, the tree towers over daily crowds enjoying the sights and sounds of Christmas in one of the world's great cities. As children scamper around and over the lions, bands of carolers gather nightly before the tree, singing beloved old hymns. In the background stands St. Martin in the Fields, a church dating to 1724 that is famed for its music program, particularly its Christmas concerts.

As the crowd disperses, people walk through the streets, enjoying the holiday decorations. Traditional gaslit arcades tempt passers-by with glittering displays, shop windows offer holiday panoramas, and lighted Christmas trees brighten many storefronts.

The magic of shop windows

The famous department store Harrods, an entire block long and completely outlined in white lights, resembles an enchanted castle. The store is immense. More than 300 departments fill 7 floors. Books, clothes, perfume, furniture, silver, leather goods, and more form dazzling arrays on every floor. In the palatial

Opposite: *Trafalgar Square's famous Christmas tree has been an annual gift to London from Oslo, Norway, since 1947—a token of gratitude for British support of Norway during World War II.*

Thousands of lights adorn London's famed Harrods department store during the Christmas season.

The feet of the Wizard of Oz's *melting "wicked witch of the east" attract attention to Harrods Christmas window displays, justly famous for being highly imaginative and offbeat.*

An allée of trees, glowing blue in seasonal dress, draws visitors to the city's newest attraction—the London Eye. The huge Ferris wheel—443 feet (135 meters) tall and 394 feet (120 meters) in diameter—offers a breathtaking panorama of the city.

food halls, vast selections of meats, fish, poultry, fruits, and vegetables vie for attention with delicate pastries, ornate cakes, and delectable candies.

Children urge their parents toward the third floor, where the toy department does its best to fulfill the wistful dreams of wide-eyed youngsters. An entire section is devoted to "cuddly" toys, including bears dressed up in their holiday best.

All these offerings are for the people on one's shopping list—but what about the pets? The selection of live poultry Harrods offered in 1917 has evolved over the years into a pet shop with spa treatments and the latest fashions for that special canine or feline.

Crowds also gather at Selfridges, a large department store in London's Oxford Street. Spectators line the sidewalks to see the magic the designers have created for the window scenes. Each year, the windows are decorated in a different theme. Traditional children's stories—such as Pinocchio, with a doll-sized village full of characters from the old tale—have given way to more sophisticated displays. One year, moving Santas eat sushi, have a

A Hamley's employee uses bubble guns to lure Christmas shoppers into the company's flagship London toy store.

London's famed food emporium Fortnum & Mason is decked out for the holidays in a fashion appropriate for an institution in business since 1707. At Christmas, staff members trade their black morning coats for seasonally appropriate red ones.

beard-trim, and enjoy a bubble bath. Another year, state-of-the-art touch screens control White Christmas-themed displays that play reengineered carols.

Such London toy stores as Hamley's capture children's attention with a wealth of treasures: dolls of every size and description, stacks of games, traditional tin toy soldiers, and the latest electronic wonders. Inside the store are even more alluring offerings: wooden rocking horses standing ready for small riders; splendid dollhouses furnished in Victorian style, down to the tiniest tufted red velvet sofa; and stuffed animals sitting on shelves and counters.

The famed food emporium Fortnum & Mason on Piccadilly is especially intriguing during the holidays. Thick red carpeting muffles footsteps, pyramids of delicious foods catch the eye, and busy clerks scurry about dressed in festive red jackets. The rest of the year, the clerks dress more somberly in morning coats and striped trousers.

In the days before Christmas

In London's neighborhoods and suburbs, a short train ride from the center of the city, groups of carolers dressed in colorful costumes perform as they make their way along the High Street. People hurry by, laden with packages, bunches of glossy green holly, and Christmas trees. Families may stop briefly at a church so the children can see the crib, or manger scene. The traditional figures of Joseph and Mary are poised in the miniature Nativity, awaiting the arrival of the Infant Jesus on Christmas Eve. Camels, donkeys, and the three Wise Men in their richly colored robes are arranged beside the stable.

Shoppers completing last-minute errands—buying a turkey or choosing a Christmas tree—are greeted by Christmas decorations on wires across streets: giant, lacy snowflakes or pennants that resemble ancient woven tapestries. At the local butcher shop, pale plucked turkeys and geese hang upside down from the walls. Will it be a fat goose or a plump, fresh turkey this year? Both are traditional British Christmas fare.

Outside the greengrocer's, a small forest of cut fir trees stands on the sidewalk. Most are spruce, the British favorite for Christmas decorating.

In the days before Christmas, everyone in the family may pitch in to help make the holiday pudding. Eggs, flour, fat, spices, and raisins are all measured out and placed into a large bowl. Originally, this very rich Christmas dessert was called plum pudding and was made with prunes, or dried plums. Today, most cooks use raisins. All the family members take turns stirring, each one making a wish as they do so. Then the

Shoppers pick up last-minute gifts at London's Southbank Christmas market in the shadow of Big Ben.

For little ones, trimming the tree is one of the best days of the year.

children carefully wrap a five-penny piece in paper and drop it into the mixture. Whoever finds the coin at Christmas dinner will have good luck in the coming year, according to tradition. Some families make their pudding as much as three months before Christmas because, stored correctly, the flavor matures. The pudding, wrapped in a cloth, is steamed for two or three hours. It is traditional to bring a whole pudding to the dining table, pour brandy or rum over it, then serve it flaming.

Decking the halls

When the shopping is done, it is time to trim the tree. Out come the boxes holding the family's treasured ornaments and strings of colored lights. The tree is fitted into its stand and placed in a corner of the living room. It fills the room with its fresh, woodsy scent.

Shiny balls, glittery butterflies, colorful birds, toy soldiers, and little toy drums—all made of molded glass—are hung from the branches. Children make garlands of brightly colored, twisted streamers and fling silvery tinsel onto the tree. Finally the last decoration is placed—the special angel, fairy, or star that goes on the top of the tree.

Some families exchange Christmas cards with friends and distant loved ones, and these may be hung on long strings on the mantle or across doorways. Sprigs of evergreen may also adorn the fireplace mantel. Shimmering garlands may hang from the ceiling.

Father Christmas

Finally, it's time for the children's annual letter to Father Christmas. A list of desired presents is carefully printed on a scrap of paper and tossed onto the flames in the fireplace. Father Christmas somehow manages to read the request as the smoke and ashes rise out of the chimney.

Today, Father Christmas is the British name for Santa Claus. But long ago in England, the spirit of Yuletide revelry was based on a different figure called Father Christmas. The old Father Christmas wore a wreath of mistletoe or holly upon his head, and his robe was usually green. He represented the coming of spring.

The Father Christmas of today was influenced by the Santa Claus ("Sinterklaas") that Dutch settlers brought with them to

Over time, Britain's Father Christmas—garbed in green and wearing a crown of holly—morphed into an Americanized Santa Claus figure.

the New World in the 1800's. Over the years, that figure turned into the jovial, fat grandfather figure who dresses in red and delivers gifts in a reindeer-drawn sleigh.

The Santa figure that began to appear in the United Kingdom in the 1900's was a mixture of America's merry sprite and the old Father Christmas. He is usually pictured as rather thin and tall, with a white beard, and wearing a long crimson robe with a hood or cap trimmed in white fur. At Christmastime, many British department stores have either a Father Christmas or a Santa Claus who listens to children's wishes. Every child falls asleep on Christmas Eve wondering how Father Christmas is able to read smoke and ashes.

Christmas Eve

The day before Christmas is a busy time. There are presents still to be wrapped and placed beneath the tree and last-minute

Skaters enjoy a crisp winter's night on an ice rink in the courtyard of Somerset House, an 18th-century London landmark.

A senior citizen chorus sings carols in a London neighborhood. The singing of carols takes place all over London in the days before Christmas.

Children generally hang the stockings the last thing before going to bed on Christmas Eve.

baking to be done. The children may be sent out to ice skate on a nearby rink or pond. When they come home for tea, the tree is surrounded by even higher piles of gifts.

After supper on Christmas Eve, in many British families it is the custom for each child to open one small gift. Then the family may listen to the many bands of carolers being televised from all over London. Groups sing in great cathedrals, in crowded and lively pubs, outside the Tower of London, and even on barges on the River Thames.

Finally, it is time for children to hang stockings over the fireplace. Then it is time for bed, often with the reading of a chapter or two from everyone's favorite Christmas story, Charles Dickens's *A Christmas Carol* (1843).

16 Christmas in the United Kingdom

Christmas Past

No other people have observed Christmas with more enthusiasm than the English—and they have been celebrating it for well over 1,000 years! According to legend, King Arthur spent Christmas at York in the year 521 with "jocund [merry] guests, minstrels, gleemen, harpers, pipe-players, jugglers, and dancers." According to one English chronicle, King Arthur, his clergy, all his nobility, soldiers, and neighbors spent the holidays in mirth, jollity, and drinking.

Except for a brief period of Puritan rule, vigorous feasting and merrymaking have ever since been the order of the season. Even the word *Christmas* comes from *Christes* (Christ) and *Masse,* an old English word for feast or festival. Once, Christmas was celebrated for 12 days each year, each day having its own name and special observances.

Early invaders of England came from many parts of Europe, and they brought their own customs with them. Christianity arrived in England in the 500's A.D., and eventually Christmas became a merry fusion of old and new, of pagan and Christian rituals.

The Middle Ages

In the Middle Ages (A.D. 400's to 1500), everyone, upper and lower classes alike, enjoyed the merriest of holidays. Noble lords and ladies held open house. There were Yule log ceremonies, jousting tournaments, spectacular pageants, and much feasting and drinking.

By the 900's and 1000's, many nobles lived in castles. They entertained in a public room known as the great hall. There, rushes were spread loosely over the stone floor. A high ceiling loomed above. Intricate tapestries of enormous size covered the walls to keep out drafts, and an immense fireplace dominated the room, giving off heat and light.

At a banquet such as a Christmas feast, men and women dressed in their best clothes, made of rich, jewel-toned fabrics. Dinner began about noon, and the meal went on for hours. Accompanied by a blaring fanfare of trumpets, a long procession

Opposite: *Warwick Castle, begun by William the Conqueror in 1068, stands at a bend in the River Avon in Warwickshire.*

A village teems with activity as its inhabitants observe the traditions in a depiction of an English Christmas Eve in about 1460. A choir sings carols; boys drag in the Yule log; others decorate a home with holly and othr greenery, including a kissing bough; and the lady of the manor prepares to store the Twelfth Night cake.

would enter the hall. First might come a lady bearing a tray upon which reposed a whole peacock—skinned, roasted, and with the plumage put back—its beak gilded and its tail feathers arranged in a fan of iridescent splendor.

Then, the master cook would march in, surrounded by cheering onlookers. He proudly carried a silver tray bearing the head of a boar festively decorated with holly and rosemary sprigs, an orange in its mouth. In those days, wild boars were common in England's thick forests. They were dangerous beasts. According to one story, a student at Oxford University went off to study in the forest one day and was attacked by a boar. To save himself, the young man shoved his copy of Aristotle down the animal's throat and choked it to death. He brought the boar's head back to school, where it was duly roasted and eaten. The book was saved, too. Even today at Queen's College, Oxford, they celebrate the ancient Boar's Head Ceremony. The choir sings a traditional carol, and the chief singer is presented with the orange from the boar's mouth.

A feast for kings

Kings in those times were quite accustomed to giving sumptuous banquets. Henry III (1207-1272) ordered 600 oxen slaughtered for Christmas in 1252. King Richard II (1367-1400) was said to have employed 2,000 cooks. It is recorded that he fed 10,000 people every day, let alone at Christmas! And Henry VII (1457-1509) offered his guests 120 dishes for one holiday feast.

Even in those days, the meal was topped off with plum pudding, though it was not the round and hard confection made today. In the Middle Ages, it was a soupy dish made of mutton broth, dried fruit, and spices. Cooks did not begin to boil it to make it hard until the 1600's—and, of course, the recipe has changed somewhat since then.

Guests at a noble Christmas celebration lounged at long, wooden tables as servants ran to and fro bringing dishes of food or refilling goblets with ale and mead. Other servants carried in long iron spits with chunks of roasted meat. Dogs crouched nearby, ready to snap up a tasty morsel of food tossed by the diners. The dogs also had another purpose: Guests often wiped their greasy fingers on the fur of a dog lying at their feet. No one used forks in those days; they were developed later and were considered a luxury.

The traditional Boar's Head Ceremony at Queen's College, Oxford, is depicted in a 19th-century engraving.

Servants prepare a sumptuous Christmas feast in an artist's rendering of a 17th-century kitchen in a noble household.

The feast (clockwise, from far upper right) includes lemon mincemeat; beef and samphire hash; scorched chestnuts; buttered oranges; pigeon pie; sillabub—a desert based on milk or cream; crystallized flowers and herbs; harts horn flummery—a jelly made with shavings from the soft velvet antlers of young male deer; and turkey garnished with mushrooms, truffles, and sweetmeats.

The only light inside a castle was from the fireplace and from dozens of candles. Poorer people lit their homes with bundles of rushes dipped in melted tallow fat, which produced a great deal of smoke.

During the feast, minstrels strolled about entertaining the guests. A jester performed somersaults and cartwheels, bells jingling merrily on his cap. Jugglers tossed objects into the air, deftly caught them, and sent them soaring again. At some point,

A great cheer is raised as men drag the Yule log into the fire as depicted in a 19th-century engraving. By tradition, the Yule log burned throughout the Christmas season. What remained of the log was saved to be used to start the new log at the next Christmas season.

a band of servants would drag a gigantic oak log into the hall—the Yule log. As one end of the log was ceremoniously pushed into the fireplace, everyone in the vast hall broke into song. Scandinavian invaders brought the custom to England, and it became an annual tradition. The log was meant to burn all through the Christmas season, and the bits left over were kept to start the new log the following year.

The Lord of Misrule leads a merry group of villagers in a 16th century procession as depicted in a 19th century engraving.

The Lord of Misrule

As the guests ate, an imposing gentleman in tights and rainbow-hued costume would stalk about the hall, waving his hand in regal gestures as if directing the proceedings. He wore a swooping hat with long peacock feathers attached to the crown. A huge ruffled collar circled his neck, and an ermine-bordered cape fell from his shoulders. A small page boy followed him, holding up the end of the cape so it would not drag on the rush-strewn floor. The figure was known as the Lord of Misrule, a pagan master of ceremonies of sorts for the Christmas revels. The custom began in ancient

A jester and his monkeys perform as servers present guests with courses of heron and peacock in an artist's rendering of a medieval Christmas feast.

Rome, long before the birth of Christ, when the Romans celebrated a great feast around the time of the winter solstice, the shortest day of the year.

The Romans called their festival the Saturnalia. On that day, everything was turned topsy-turvy; the social order was reversed. Masters served their slaves, men and women exchanged clothing, and grotesque masks were worn, even on the streets. This upside-down manner of celebrating turned up again in England during the Middle Ages as part of the Christmas festivities. Kings and nobles chose Lords of

Misrule to reign over the entire holiday season, from Christmas to Twelfth Night.

A Lord of Misrule used all of his imagination—and large quantities of the noble's money—to think up games and amusing things to do. Everything had to be the exact opposite of normal, everyday life. Continuous merriment was the rule. Even kings and queens had to obey the Christmas Lords' orders, and they did!

The custom continued for hundreds of years. Henry VII and Henry VIII (1491-1547) both loved it, as did Queen Elizabeth I (1533-1603). Although the rowdy, uproarious revelry caused by the Lord of Misrule was enormously popular, it was severely frowned upon by the Church, and eventually the practice died out.

Christmas in the Middle Ages was one long, boisterous round of gaiety. Besides the feasting, drinking, singing, and dancing, people hunted, gambled, watched plays, and attended lavish tournaments.

Knights were invited to come from all over the kingdom, even from western Europe, to compete. One Christmas in the 1300's, Richard II held a tournament in which the pageantry and the tilting contests—dueling on horseback—lasted for almost two weeks. On the opening day, heralds and minstrels accompanied the courageous knights, and each challenger was led in by a young lady on horseback who held a silver chain attached to the knight's neck.

Christmas celebrations in the Middle Ages often included tournaments, where knights jousted to prove their strength and for the entertainment of the nobles.

A ban on Christmas

In 1649, a group of people called Puritans, led by Oliver Cromwell, took over the country. The Puritans were members of a religious and social movement of the 1500's and 1600's who considered the Bible as the true law of God, which provided guidelines for government led by church leaders. The Puritans felt that the old ways of celebrating Christmas and other holidays had gotten out of hand, and Parliament abolished all religious festivities. Christmas was to be just another working day. The people rebelled. There were riots, and one mayor was beaten senseless by a mob. But the government held firm and, slowly, Christmas nearly disappeared, at least on the surface. Most people still celebrated secretly, but there was no more wild merrymaking.

The Puritans even went so far as to ban mince pies. At one time, mince pies were baked in an oblong shape, to look like a manger. They often had a little image of the Christ Child on top. The Puritans considered this irreligious. So mince pies went into hiding, too. Later, folks began to bake them again, but they were round and much smaller.

Christmas in Britain was banned when the monarchy was overthrown and the government was taken over by Puritans led by Oliver Cromwell in 1649. Festivities resumed—though not on so grand a scale— after the monarchy was restored in 1660.

Kissing boughs, mistletoe, and holly

The ban on Christmas ended after the monarchy was restored in 1660. Although the holiday subsequently became more spiritual, it retained certain elements of its pagan past. Holiday parties often included dancing. Men and women leapt about energetically, jigging to lively tunes played by a perspiring fiddler. A large globe made of two hoops covered with holly and other greenery hung from the rafters. Ribbons, apples, and burning candles were attached to it, and a sprig of mistletoe dangled from it. Each time a couple danced beneath the globe, the man gave his partner a resounding kiss. The globe was called a "kissing bough," and it was a tradition to hang one in the home before there were Christmas trees.

Mistletoe was the sacred plant of the Druids, a priestly class among the Celts, an ancient people of Europe. Druidism was practiced until about the 400's, when most of the Celts became

Christians. The Druids called mistletoe "all-heal," because they believed it could cure illnesses. It also protected people from witches. The Druids used a golden sickle to cut mistletoe down from the trees on which it grew. Years later, Christians forbade the use of mistletoe in churches because it was associated with the Druids and their often cruel pagan customs.

Holly was also reputed to be able to ward off witches. Bringing holly and ivy into the house at Christmastime is an ancient custom, dating back to the Roman winter celebrations. The early Christians thought that holly resembled Christ's crown of thorns with its sharp-needled leaves and blood-red berries. Ivy, on the other hand, was a symbol of Bacchus, the Roman god of wine. Long ago, holly was supposed to

Before the British adopted the German tradition of decorating a Christmas tree, they hung "kissing boughs" in their homes. A kissing bough was shaped like a globe, covered in holly and other greenery, and included a sprig of mistletoe.

Tradition demanded that couples kiss as they danced under the kissing bough, as depicted in a 19th-century illustration from Charles Dickens's The Pickwick Papers.

represent man, and ivy represented woman. An old tradition said that if the Christmas holly was prickly, the master would rule the household for the coming year. If the holly leaves were smooth, then the mistress would rule.

The Victorian Era

During the Victorian Era—the reign of Queen Victoria (1837-1901)—some new touches were added to the holiday season, including the Christmas tree and Christmas cards. Christmas trees were not an English invention. They came from Germany. Queen Victoria's husband, Prince Albert, was German. After Albert and Victoria married in 1840, he shared his country's custom with his young English wife.

But Victoria's Christmas tree was not the first in England. Others had already appeared, as far back as the beginning of the century. However, it was not until word spread about the queen's trees that the idea was taken up by ordinary people. Everyone wanted to imitate royalty's newfangled notion. Charles Dickens (1812-1870) called it "that pretty German toy." Before many years had passed, Christmas trees could be found in households all over England.

A robin is a traditional British Christmas motif, appearing often on greeting cards. Joseph is said to have built a fire in the manger to keep Mary and Jesus warm, but the flames kept dying. To keep the fire going, a robin fanned it with its wings, burning his breast fiery red. According to another tradition, a robin plucked thorns from the brow of Jesus as He carried the Cross. His blood forever stained the bird's breast red.

Victorian Christmas trees, like those today, often had a star or an angel with outstretched wings perched at the top. Exquisite little baskets and trays filled with candies and fruits hung from the branches. Fancy cakes and gilded gingerbread figures were also tied to the branches with colored ribbons.

Christmas inspired many writers and poets, too, and some of the liveliest examples of Christmas literature have come from England. William Shakespeare, John Milton, Robert Herrick, Lord Tennyson, William Makepeace Thackeray, Anthony

Queen Victoria and Prince Albert and their children appear in an illustration from a December 1848 edition of the London News. *Victoria's German-born husband is credited with popularizing the German tradition of the Christmas tree in Britain.*

Trollope, Christina Rossetti—these and many more have given us the flavor, taste, and sound of British Christmastide.

Charles Dickens, sometimes called "Father Christmas himself," toured England and America several times, giving readings of *A Christmas Carol*, as well as other works. Eager audiences stood in long lines in freezing weather to hear him. Perhaps no other piece of literature has influenced our idea of what a traditional Christmas should be as much as Dickens's *A Christmas Carol* (1843). The warmth and love shared by the hard-working Cratchit family and the goodness of Tiny Tim shine forth in the following chapter from Dickens's famous novel.

Christmas at the Cratchits'

Then up rose Mrs. Cratchit, Cratchit's wife, dressed out but poorly in a twice-turned gown, but brave in ribbons, which are cheap and make a goodly show for sixpence; and she laid the cloth, assisted by Belinda Cratchit, second of her daughters, also brave in ribbons; while Master Peter Cratchit plunged a fork into the saucepan of potatoes, and getting the corners of his monstrous shirt collar (Bob's private property, conferred upon his son and heir in honour of the day) into his mouth, rejoiced to find himself so gallantly attired, and yearned to show his linen in the fashionable Parks. And now two smaller Cratchits, boy and girl, came tearing in, screaming that outside the baker's they had smelt the goose, and known it for their own; and basking in luxurious thoughts of sage and onion, these young Cratchits danced about the table, and exalted Master

Peter Cratchit to the skies, while he (not proud, although his collars nearly choked him) blew the fire until the slow potatoes bubbling up, knocked loudly at the saucepan-lid to be let out and peeled.

"What has ever got your precious father, then?" said Mrs. Cratchit. "And your brother, Tiny Tim! And Martha warn't as late last Christmas Day by half-an-hour!"

"Here's Martha, mother!" said a girl, appearing as she spoke.

"Here's Martha, mother!" cried the two young Cratchits. "Hurrah! There's such a goose, Martha!"

"Why, bless your heart alive, my dear, how late you are!" said Mrs. Cratchit, kissing her a dozen times, and taking off her shawl and bonnet for her with officious zeal.

"We'd a deal of work to finish up last night," replied the girl, "and had to clear away this morning, mother!"

"Well! Never mind so long as you are come," said Mrs. Cratchit. "Sit ye down before the fire, my dear, and have a warm, Lord bless ye!"

"No, no! There's father coming," cried the two young Cratchits, who were everywhere at once. "Hide, Martha, hide!"

So Martha hid herself, and in came little Bob, the father, with at least three feet of comforter exclusive of the fringe hanging down before him; and his threadbare clothes darned up and brushed, to look seasonable; and Tiny Tim upon his shoulder. Alas for Tiny Tim, he bore a little crutch and had his limbs supported by an iron frame!

"Why, where's our Martha?" cried Bob Cratchit, looking round.

"Not coming," said Mrs. Cratchit.

"Not coming!" said Bob, with a sudden declension in his high spirits; for he had been Tim's blood horse all the way from church and had come home rampant. "Not coming upon Christmas Day!"

Martha didn't like to see him disappointed, if it were only in joke; so she came out prematurely from behind the closed door, and ran into his arms, while the two young Cratchits hustled Tiny Tim, and bore him off into the wash-house, that he might hear the pudding singing in the copper.

"And how did little Tim behave?" asked Mrs. Cratchit, when she had rallied Bob on his credulity and Bob had hugged his daughter to his heart's content.

"As good as gold," said Bob, "and better. Somehow he gets thoughtful sitting by himself so much, and thinks the

strangest things you ever heard. He told me coming home, that he hoped the people saw him in the church, because he was a cripple, and it might be pleasant to them to remember upon Christmas Day, who made lame beggars walk and blind men see."

Bob's voice was tremulous when he told them this, and trembled more when he said that Tiny Tim was growing strong and hearty.

His active little crutch was heard upon the floor, and back came Tiny Tim before another word was spoken, escorted by his brother and sister to his stool before the fire;

and while Bob, turning up his cuffs—as if, poor fellow, they were capable of being made more shabby—compounded some hot mixture in a jug with gin and lemons, and stirred it round and round and put it on the hob to simmer; Master Peter and the two ubiquitous young Cratchits went to fetch the goose, with which they soon returned in high procession.

Such a bustle ensued that you might have thought a goose the rarest of all birds; a feathered phenomenon, to which a black swan was a matter of course—and in truth it was something very like it in that house. Mrs. Cratchit made the gravy (ready beforehand in a little saucepan) hissing hot; Master Peter mashed the potatoes with incredible vigour; Miss Belinda sweetened up the applesauce; Martha dusted the hot plates; Bob took Tiny

Tim beside him in a tiny corner at the table; the two young Cratchits set chairs for everybody, not forgetting themselves, and mounting guard upon their posts crammed spoons into their mouths lest they should shriek for goose before their turn came to be helped. At last the dishes were set on, and grace was said. It was succeeded by a breathless pause, as Mrs. Cratchit, looking slowly all along the carving knife, prepared to plunge it in the breast; but when she did, and when the long expected gush of stuffing issued forth, one murmur of delight arose all around the board, and even Tiny Tim, excited by the two young Cratchits, beat on the table with the handle of his knife, and feebly cried Hurrah!

There never was such a goose. Bob said he didn't believe there ever was such a goose cooked. Its tenderness and flavour, size and cheapness, were the themes of universal

admiration. Eked out by the applesauce and mashed potatoes, it was a sufficient dinner for the whole family; indeed, as Mrs. Cratchit said with great delight (surveying one small atom of a bone upon the dish) they hadn't ate it all at last! Yet everyone had had enough, and the youngest Cratchits in particular were steeped in sage and onion to the eyebrows! But now, the plates being changed by Miss Belinda, Mrs. Cratchit left the room alone—too nervous to bear witnesses—to take the plum pudding up and bring it in.

Suppose it should not be done enough! Suppose it should break in turning out! Suppose somebody should have got over the wall of the backyard, and stolen it, while they were merry with the goose—a supposition at which the two young Cratchits became livid! All sorts of horrors were supposed.

Hallo! A great deal of steam! The pudding was out of the copper. A smell like washing-day! That was the cloth. A smell like an eating-house and pastry cook's next door to each other, with a laundress's next door to that! That was the pudding! In half a minute Mrs. Cratchit entered—flushed, but smiling proudly—with the pudding, like a speckled cannonball, so hard and firm, blazing in half of half-a-quartern of ignited brandy, and bedight with Christmas holly stuck into the top.

Oh, a wonderful pudding! Bob Cratchit said, and calmly too, that he regarded it as the greatest success achieved by Mrs. Cratchit since their marriage. Mrs. Cratchit said that now the weight was off her mind, she would confess she had had her doubts about the quantity of flour. Everybody had something to say about it, but nobody said or thought it was at all a small pudding for a large family. It would have been flat heresy to do so. Any Cratchit would have blushed to hint at such a thing.

At last the dinner was all done, the cloth was cleared, the hearth swept, and the fire made up. The compound in the jug being tasted, and considered perfect, apples and oranges were put upon the table, and a shovelful of chestnuts on the fire. Then all the Cratchit family drew around the hearth, in what Bob Cratchit called a circle, meaning half a one; and at Bob's elbow stood the family display of glass. Two tumblers and a custard-cup without a handle.

These held the hot stuff from the jug, however, as well as golden goblets would have done; and Bob served it out with beaming looks, while the chestnuts on the fire sputtered and cracked noisily. Then Bob proposed:—

"A Merry Christmas to us all, my dears. God bless us!"

Which all the family re-echoed.

"God bless us every one!" said Tiny Tim, the last of all.

Presents, Parties and Pantomimes

Stockings come first on Christmas morning in Britain. Still heavy-eyed with sleep, children tumble out of bed and race for the fireplace. The stockings, empty the night before, are now magically lumpy and misshapen—but not for long. There may be a miniature Paddington Bear, dressed in yellow boots and slicker; oranges, nuts, and candies; tiny puzzles or games; or other small treats. Finally, it is time to open the gifts under the tree. In short order, the living room is littered with torn wrapping paper, empty boxes, and gifts. There are games and books, a new sweater for Dad, an antique pewter bowl for Mum, and much, much more.

While many people attend midnight services on Christmas Eve, others go to church on Christmas morning. Massive Gothic cathedrals and small village churches resound with the joyous pealing of bells and voices raised in song. Altars, walls, and pews are decorated with fir branches. Rows of flickering candles and Christmas trees brighten the dark shadows.

At home, the family gathers for Christmas dinner. A tempting roast turkey, fat with stuffing, waits to be carved. Surrounding it may be little sausages, Brussels sprouts, and roast potatoes. A bowl of steaming giblet gravy sits close to the turkey. Dishes full of nuts and candies are scattered over the table, and there is a large Stilton cheese, to be sampled later.

The grand finale—the Christmas pudding—will be presented at the end of the meal. Holly sprigs may adorn it, and flames of burning brandy blaze over its rounded surface. Portions are served with either cream or a hard sauce (a sweet, liquor-flavored sauce).

A cracker at every place

At the table, "crackers," decorated tubes made with twisted paper, are found beside each plate. Crackers are an indispensable part of holiday celebrations in Britain. They come in a

Opposite: Christmas Eve service at St. Peter's Church in Bournemouth, England

It's Christmas morning, and the little ones are amazed to see the treasures Father Christmas has left under the tree.

Everyone waits for the "crack" of the bursting crackers as they reveal the riddles, hats, and small toys hidden inside. Christmas crackers have been a tradition in the United Kingdom since the mid-1800's.

A family enjoys Christmas dinner "donned in gay apparel," the traditional paper crowns found in crackers. The holiday turkey is often accompanied by ham, brussels sprouts, and a host of side dishes.

wide range of shiny colors. They are decorated with tiny silver bells or paper flowers or holly. The ends may be plain or made of lacy paper. They are usually small, but one can find giant crackers that are several feet long. Crackers produce a loud bang and break apart when the ends are pulled.

Tucked inside are silly paper hats and crowns, small toys, and slips of paper with funny riddles printed on them. They are not just for children—grown-ups also enjoy popping the crackers, putting on the hats, and reading the riddles. The crowns may symbolize the Three Wise Men who came to see the Infant Jesus.

The Queen's speech
At 3 p.m., families throughout the land turn on the "telly"— the television—or the radio or connect to the Internet to

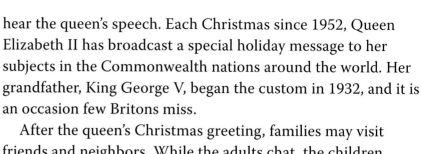

hear the queen's speech. Each Christmas since 1952, Queen Elizabeth II has broadcast a special holiday message to her subjects in the Commonwealth nations around the world. Her grandfather, King George V, began the custom in 1932, and it is an occasion few Britons miss.

After the queen's Christmas greeting, families may visit friends and neighbors. While the adults chat, the children play games. Traditional Christmas games may include Pass Around the Parcel. Children sit in a circle and pass a wrapped parcel from child to child. Music is played as the package goes around, and the kids clap their hands in time to the song. When the music stops, the lucky child holding the parcel is the winner and gets to keep the present inside.

In a centuries-old game called Hot Cockles, one person kneels or lays face down in the center of the room and is blindfolded. The others in turn tap him on the shoulder, and he tries to guess who has tapped him. If he guesses correctly, that person takes his place in the center. A letter containing a reference to the game was printed in a magazine in 1711: "I am a Footman in a great Family and am in love with the House-maid. We were all at Hot-cockles last Night in the Hall these Holidays; when I lay down and was blinded,

A family makes short work of the gifts under the tree.

she pull'd off her shoe, and hit me with the Heel such a Rap, as almost broke my Head to Pieces. Pray, Sir, was this Love or Spite?"

A long-time favorite is charades. One team acts out the title of a book or movie, or perhaps a well-known saying. The other team tries to guess what it is.

Before turning in for the night, some families prepare an old-fashioned bowl of wassail, a kind of punch. Hot ale is poured into a large punch bowl. Eggs, spices, and sugar are added. Finally, a few small roasted apples are tossed in, making a hissing noise as they bob about in the steaming liquid. The word *wassail* was originally a Scandinavian term brought to England by the Vikings. *Was hael* meant *good health*. People toasted each other with this drink. Sometimes it was also called "lamb's wool." This name may refer to wishing one another a good harvest of wool from sheared sheep that was central to the economy of England in the Middle Ages.

Queen Elizabeth II delivers her Christmas greeting to the Commonwealth nations on Christmas Day. The speech is filmed in great secrecy either at Buckingham Palace, Windsor Castle, or Sandringham—the queen's private country house, where the royal family spends Christmas.

Boxing Day

The British enjoy a post-Christmas holiday besides New Year—Boxing Day, which falls either on December 26 or on the first weekday after Christmas. Boxing Day has a long history. The day after Christmas is also St. Stephen's Day. Long ago, churches had special boxes for contributions at Christmas services. The boxes were opened on St. Stephen's Day, and the money inside was distributed to the poor. People began calling the day Boxing Day sometime in the Middle Ages. Later, the poor started to go around to wealthy households on that day to collect money. Then it became the custom to give presents of clothes, food, or

money to delivery boys and to such people as the milkman, chimney sweep, or postman on Boxing Day. Even though the money was by then usually given in an envelope, the gift was still called a Christmas box.

In many parts of the United Kingdom, a fox hunt has long been a traditional Boxing Day event. Although fox hunting was banned by the Hunting Act in 2004, many people still turn out for meets, often to simply watch the grand pageantry. Ladies and gentlemen wearing black coats or bright hunting pink (which is actually red) sit astride sleek horses. A pack of brown and white

A fox hunt begins near Bicester, England, on Boxing Day, the day after Christmas. The hunting of foxes with dogs was banned by the Hunting Act of 2004. However, the tradition lives on in hunts during which dogs follow the scent without killing the fox.

hounds mills about, baying excitedly. Stirrup cups, the customary pre-hunt drink, are passed up to the riders. Some groups in England continue to seek to overturn the fox hunting ban, which is often considered unenforceable.

Boxing Day is also the big day for football (the European term for soccer) in Britain. Motor car races are popular, too.

Pantomimes

After Boxing Day, the most important Christmastime event for many families is going to see a pantomime. The Christmas pantomime is a uniquely British production. To Americans, pantomime means acting with the body, without words. In Britain, it is a lot more and great fun for children and adults alike.

In large cities, especially London, top television and stage personalities star in pantomimes. These are lavish extrava-

Captain Hook from "Peter Pan" and Fairy Bowbells from "Dick Whittington" appear together at the Piccadilly Theatre in London during an event to launch the Christmas pantomime season. Attending a pantomime is a favorite holiday activity for many families in the United Kingdom.

ganzas, elaborately produced and filled with silly jokes, songs, and such well-known gags as the custard pie in the face. Traditionally, there is a "dame" who is played by a man. The "principal boy" used to be played by a girl wearing tights—quite a daring move during the Victorian Age. Nowadays, the role may be acted by either male or female.

The stories are spoofs of old fairy tales, with comments on current events thrown in. Cinderella, Puss in Boots, Jack and the Beanstalk, and similar tales have all been favorite pantomimes for years. Over time, such new ones as Peter Pan and Aladdin have been added, as were the fairy tales of Danish author Hans Christian Andersen.

Men portraying women— or "dames"—in extravagant, over-the-top fashion is a standard part of the uniquely British style of pantomime.

Lively interaction between the players and the audience is expected. Characters on stage call out to the kids in the theater, and the children yell right back! The audience "boos" the villain, warns the hero "it's behind you!" and urges the young man to "kiss her, kiss her" when the heroine appears.

The British style of pantomime is probably rooted in *commedia dell'arte*, a type of comedy that became popular in Italy in the 1500's. In *commedia dell'arte*, the actors made up dialogue as they went along.

Modern English pantomime dates from the early 1700's. John Rich, owner, actor, and manager of Lincoln's Inn Fields Theatre in London, produced one of the first, in 1717. Like all the pantomimes to follow, the performance included a wondrous "transformation" in which huts and cottages turned into palaces, and just about everything on stage—even the actors—seemed to become something else. It was so well received that Rich eventually presented and performed in pantomimes at three theaters—Covent Garden, Drury Lane, and his own—for the next 43 years.

A manger scene is displayed at York Minster, a huge Gothic cathedral in York, England. During the Epiphany, the Wise Men appear before the creche.

Afternoon tea

The rest of the holiday season may be spent in visiting friends and family, where the guests may be served a traditional tea—finger sandwiches with thin slices of cucumber or salmon; hot, buttery scones with jam and clotted cream; fruit-filled tarts; and the special holiday treat, the Christmas cake. Rich and dark with fruit and nuts, covered with a layer of marzipan and then thickly frosted, the cake is always a smashing success.

There are also small, tart-sized mince pies with brandy butter. At one time, it was the custom to eat one mince pie on each of the twelve days of Christmas. According to tradition, the practice would bring good luck for all the months of the year.

From New Year's Day to Twelfth Night

At one time in England, gifts were given on New Year's Day rather than Christmas. In Elizabethan times, ladies-in-waiting,

the royal physician, even the master cook all gave the queen, Elizabeth I (1533-1603), gifts, such as gowns, jewelry, or candy. She loved sweets, especially marzipan molded into all kinds of shapes—even a chessboard, one year. Her subjects did not always give these presents voluntarily. She "requested" them, and no one dared refuse.

Twelfth Night, January 5, marks the end of the Christmas season in the United Kingdom. It is time to take down the Christmas decorations. Holly and Christmas cards are removed, the ornaments are wrapped in tissue paper, and Christmas hopes and dreams are put away for another year. Those who do not take down their decorations risk having goblins enter their houses to leave a mess.

Contrary to this tradition, churches leave their Nativity scenes up for Epiphany celebrations on January 6. At that time, the Three Wise Men appear before the manger.

A child's new toy comes in handy for disposing of the Christmas tree. With Twelfth Night, the Christmas season ends. According to tradition, it is time to take down the tree and pack up the decorations or risk bad luck in the coming year.

Customs Throughout the Land

Christmas is a time for tradition, and a host of strange and picturesque customs of the past are still observed faithfully in the United Kingdom each year. Some are very old, dating back to pagan times or the Middle Ages. Others have come into being in more recent centuries; many are traceable to the various conquerors who came from other lands. The people who live in England, Scotland, Wales, and Northern Ireland all have their own unique ways of observing the Christmas season, and each regional custom adds another element to the merry mixture of celebrations that is British Christmas.

Play-acting has been part of English Christmastime entertainment for hundreds of years. Mystery plays, portraying episodes in the life of Christ, were popular in the Middle Ages. There were miracle plays, too, religious dramas about saints and martyrs. In the royal courts, masques were once a favorite holiday fare. These were pageant-like theatricals in verse, in which the performers dressed in elaborate costumes and masks. Kings and queens often took roles themselves, and in the 1600's several masques were written especially for the royal family by the poet and playwright Ben Jonson (1572-1637). By the 1700's, masques had disappeared, replaced by the pantomime.

The mummers' play

Another form of ancient drama still exists today in England—the mummers' play. Like the miracle and mystery plays, it was originally a folk drama, but its roots were more pagan than religious. The mummers' play celebrates the return of spring after a long winter, or the coming resurrection after death.

Customarily, only men perform the roles. They dress in fanciful costumes and either wear masks or blacken their faces. Early mummers often wore grotesque animal headdresses; some dressed in straw costumes or were covered with colored strips of paper. In most versions of the play—and there are many—the players are led in by Father Christmas, who also sets the scenes.

Opposite: *The Town Crier leads a mummers' parade on Boxing Day in Marshfield, England. The mummers carry swords with which they re-enact a play based on pagan rituals that celebrate the triumph of life over death and the return of spring after winter.*

In a mummers' play in Bampton, a family watches while a quack doctor attempts to revive a slain St. George.

The names of the characters and number of players vary widely, but certain basic types are always present.

The hero, St. George, kills a fierce dragon and fights a battle with an evil Ottoman knight. A sword dance is often part of the play, ending with the mock death of St. George. A quack doctor brings the hero back to life, and one or two comical fellows collect money from the audience. The play is all in rhyme and performed with great gusto, with songs and dances mixed in.

The Hodening horse and the Mari Lwyd

Sometimes mummers' plays include a character dressed up like a hobbyhorse. In some regions, the hobbyhorse goes about with its own procession of mummers and is called the Hodening Horse. The head is hand-carved from wood and fixed to a pole. It has two carved-out eyes and a huge jaw with large teeth, which are made to clack and snap by pulling a string. Ribbons, rosettes, and jingling bells are added for decoration. Covered with a cloth or blanket, the rider romps about astride the pole in a bent-over position so that he resembles a real horse. A lighted candle may be placed in the hollow of the head, causing the mouth to glow like a fiery furnace—a fearsome sight, especially when seen peering into a window at night!

Wales has a similar custom called Mari Lwyd. The leading mummer wears the ribbon-bedecked skull of a horse. The bizarrely costumed players visit previously selected houses and go through a kind of battle of wits with the householders. They bang loudly on the door with a stick and sing out impromptu verses; the people inside must reply with more made-up verse. If the horse and his group can outwit the host, they are invited in for cakes and cider.

The Glastonbury Thorn

According to a legend from the Middle Ages, the Glastonbury Thorn blossoms whenever a member of the royal family visits Glastonbury, in Somerset. The Vicar plucks off a bud and presents it in a silver box to the royal visitor.

The tale of the magical Thorn began many centuries ago, when St. Joseph of Arimathea was said to have come to England to preach the Gospel. (Joseph of Arimathea was a wealthy member of the ruling council in Jerusalem at the time that Jesus was crucified; Joseph offered his own tomb for Jesus's burial.) He journeyed to Glastonbury's Wearyall Hill, where, on Christmas Eve, he thrust his hawthorn staff into the ground. The staff took root and grew, and every year it blossomed at midnight on December 24. The old hawthorn was destroyed by soldiers during the Puritan era, but cuttings from it had already been planted elsewhere. One such descendant grows in the ruins of Glastonbury Abbey.

The United Kingdom is made up of England, Scotland, Wales, and Northern Ireland. The people of each of these regions have their own customs that over the years have contributed to the rich experience that is British Christmas.

In Wales, singers accompany the ribbon-bedecked head of a horse called the Mari Lwyd from house to house. At each stop, the group sings traditional Welsh songs. Welcoming the group into the home was said to bring the homeowner good luck in the new year.

In 1752, the government changed the calendar in England—eliminating 11 days! The people didn't like this one bit. The change threw the holidays out of kilter, and the English people thought that they had been robbed, somehow, of those missing days. That year, and for several years after, the Glastonbury Thorn was watched with great interest—would it flower on the old Christmas Eve, the new, or on what had been January 5? Supposedly, it bloomed on the old Christmas Eve more often than not, confirming the people's belief that the government had wickedly interfered with the true date of Christ's birth.

The Glastonbury Thorn still blooms pretty much on schedule. In 2010, vandals hacked the branches off the 50-year-old tree that had grown from a cutting on Wearyall Hill. With careful nursing, the tree recovered. A sprig from the Glastonbury Thorn is sent to the queen each Christmas, to serve as a decoration on her dinner table. The truth of the matter is that the Thorn is a flowering type that normally blooms twice a year, and one of those times is at Christmastide.

The Haxey Hood Game and Plough Stots

One Sunday in the early 1200's, it is said, Lady de Mowbray was out riding and her hood blew off. Twelve *boggans* (farmworkers) chased and recovered it. The lady was so impressed by their gallant efforts that she willed a piece of land to the village for as long as the inhabitants would reenact the event once a year. The town of Haxey, in Lincolnshire, has kept that promise. The gigantic rough-and-tumble called the Haxey Hood Game takes place there every January 6.

Costumed boggans—the "lord" and a "fool"—start off with lunch and songs at one local pub, followed by more singing at the other pub. Originally, the people then "smoked" the fool by standing him atop a pile of damp paper and straw and setting it afire. However, this proved too dangerous and was stopped.

Nowadays the group heads for a field, where 12 sack hoods are thrown up and the children try to capture them from the boggans. Later, a much larger leather hood is tossed up and a

The "fool" gets ready to start the Haxey Hood, a rough-and-tumble game that takes place each year in January in Haxey, England.

The Glastonbury Thorn (left) is said to bloom at midnight on Christmas Eve. According to legend, the tree grew from a staff thrust into the ground on Wearyall Hill in Glastonbury by Joseph of Arimathea, who offered his tomb for Christ's burial. A British postage stamp issued in 1986 (above) commemorates the legend. In truth, the hawthorn tree blooms twice a year, one of those times being around Christmas.

mad tug-of-war called the sway forms around it. Teams of men, some from neighboring villages, push and shove for several hours, until the hood is finally and victoriously carried to one of the pubs. Drinks are on the house, and the hood remains in that pub until the following year. Interested observers report that, to date, no one has been seriously injured.

The Goathland Plough Stots of North Yorkshire also perform annually in early January. *Stot* meant a bullock in old English, but somewhere along the way the word came to apply to the young men who drag a plow in the procession. A "lord" and "lady" lead off, followed by "Toms," men dressed in costumes. Sword dancers, musicians, and the plow stots come behind. Wherever the procession stops, the sword dancers go through their elegant, intricate routine, and the Toms cavort with amusing antics. A collection is taken up by "Madgy-pegs," men dressed in women's clothes, some of whom are on stilts to reach spectators in upper-story windows.

The tradition originated as a ritual based on the feast of the Epiphany, when the men of the village presented candles and other gifts to the church to ensure a good harvest in the coming year. The next day, they went door to door soliciting offerings to pay for the gifts. If anyone refused, the stots would plow a furrow in front of their home. The sword dance became a part of the ritual some years later.

Scottish New Year's customs

Although Christmas and its customs were in disfavor for only a short time in England, the government of Scotland eliminated the holiday for far longer. It was only in the 1960's that the Scots began to openly observe December 25 as a special day. But New Year's Eve—that is something else again! It's called Hogmanay and is celebrated with great enthusiasm. Revelers throng the streets of cities and towns—especially Glasgow and Edinburgh—to await the tolling of the bells that announce midnight and the New Year. Traditionally, the head of a household opens the door wide at that moment, to let out the Old Year and allow the New Year to enter.

At midnight, the custom of "first-footing" begins. Superstition has it that the first person to cross the threshold after the New Year has begun must be a dark-haired man. The reason for this is thought to go back to the days of the Viking invaders, who were usually blond or red-haired. No sensible householder would let one of those come through the door!

Also considered to be bad luck first-footers are flat-footed persons, those with eyebrows meeting over their noses, or anyone of low moral character. Women bring the worst luck of all! Because one cannot trust to chance that the right sort of person

In a celebration of their Norse heritage, revelers in Lerwick on Scotland's Shetland Islands carry flaming torches through the streets before tossing them into a Viking galley. The festival, called Up Helly Aa, takes place in late January.

will enter first, dark-haired male relatives are sometimes called upon to perform the ritual. Groups of young men often go from house to house, first-footing their friends. A lump of coal, a piece of cake, and a pinch of salt are traditional first-footers' gifts to their hosts. In return, they receive a welcoming New Year's drink.

Up Helly Aa in the Shetland Islands—the northernmost part of Scotland—is another reminder that Norsemen once ruled the land. It takes place on the last Tuesday in January and is a reenactment of the Nordic celebration of the triumph of the sun over the darkness of winter. Hundreds of men in Viking dress and horned helmets march beside a Viking galley in a torchlight procession ending at the town square. Gathering around the dragon-prowed ship, the men throw their torches into its hull. Singing a rousing traditional song, they and the fascinated onlookers watch the vessel burn, flames shooting dramatically up into the dark night sky.

"Burning out the old year" is the basis for several other ancient customs. Burning the Clavie is a New Year's Eve ritual in Burghead, Scotland. The people there use a specially prepared barrel called the clavie. They pour tar over bits of wood in the clavie and set it afire with burning peat. The person carrying the clavie thrusts his head through a hole in the barrel and staggers off with it balanced on his head and shoulders. He changes off at various points with other carriers, and bits of the clavie are

A New Year's Eve ritual in Allendale, England, involves carrying old barrels containing burning tar to the village square, where the barrels are tossed into a huge bonfire. The celebration is intended to mark the end of the old year.

handed out to the crowd for good luck. The burning tar often drips down onto the carrier—a very uncomfortable sensation, undoubtedly. The procession ends on a hill where the clavie is smashed with a hatchet.

A similar custom is practiced in Allendale, in northern England. The Tar-Barrel Parade sets forth every December 31. Men called "guisers," wearing disguises, carry "tarkits," old beer or fish barrels cut in half and filled with wood shavings covered with paraffin. The barrels are heavy, weighing 30 to 40 pounds (14 to 18 kilograms) each. Just before midnight, the procession, including a band, marches around the town and ends up at the market place. The guisers throw the tar barrels onto a huge bonfire there and sing "Auld Lang Syne" as midnight strikes.

Twelfth Night

Twelfth Night—January 5—was once surrounded by customs and legends. A Twelfth Night cake was always baked, with a bean and a pea inside. Whoever found the bean was named King of the Revels; the pea proclaimed the queen. A Twelfth Night cake is still served in the green room (the room in which actors wait to go on stage) of Drury Lane Theatre in London. Attendants wearing powdered wigs and 18th-century livery carry in the cake, courtesy of Robert Baddeley, a chef turned actor. He died in 1794, leaving £100 sterling to be invested, with the interest to be used for cake and wine for the actors to share each year in his memory.

Julie Andrews, appearing as Eliza Doolittle in the play "My Fair Lady," prepares to cut the Baddeley cake in January 1959. The cake is a Twelfth Night tradition in the green room of Drury Lane Theatre, a legacy of 18th-century chef-turned-actor Robert Baddeley, who left funds for the annual purchase of the cake for the actors.

The apple farmers of Carhampton, in Somerset, still wassail their apple trees on Old Twelfth Night (January 17) each year. Carrying guns, lanterns, and a pail of cider, they gather around a chosen tree. They place a piece of toast soaked in cider in the fork of the tree for the birds and pour more cider around the tree's roots. The men then fire their guns into the branches and toast the tree with mugs of cider and an ancient wassail song: "Here's to Thee, Old Apple Tree." The ritual is supposed to assure a good crop in the coming year.

A Joyful Noise

Mighty cathedral bells ring out in golden peals. Small handbells chime their clear, bright notes, and singers young and old carol the ancient Yuletide songs of praise and joy. Christmas in the United Kingdom is ushered in on a wave of jubilant sound!

Caroling is one of the oldest British Christmas customs, going back to the Middle Ages. Beggars at Christmastime would wander the streets of a town, singing in return for money, food, or drink. Carols were often sung between the acts of medieval mystery plays—the lovely Coventry Carol is one of these. Minstrels went from castle to castle singing Christmas songs, and in later years every town had its own band of Waits.

Waits were originally watchmen who patrolled the streets of the old walled cities. They would sing out the hours of the night, or blow notes or tunes on musical instruments. Eventually the term was applied to groups of musicians who sang and played for various civic social affairs. During the Christmas season they would make nightly rounds of the town, serenading the inhabitants. Not everyone enjoyed their services, of course. Some citizens complained bitterly of being rudely awakened from a sound sleep as the Waits caroled beneath their windows.

A-caroling we will go

Today it seems that virtually everyone in Britain goes a-caroling at Christmas. Schools, civic groups, and organizations of all sorts present programs of carols, many of them for the purpose of collecting money for charity. Carolers gather in homes, on street corners, and in every church. And caroling goes on at that pace throughout the Christmas holidays, not just on Christmas Eve.

In London, Christmas music is presented almost daily in cathedrals, concert halls, and other venues. St. Paul's Cathedral, Southwark Cathedral, St. Martin-in-the-Fields, Trafalgar Square, the Southbank Centre, Canary Wharf, Temple Church, and the Royal Albert Hall—all host concerts that start around the beginning of Advent and continue into the days between Christmas and New Year's.

Midnight services at Westminster Abbey and St. Paul's on

Opposite: Choir boys prepare for the Christmas Eve service at King's College Chapel in Cambridge. The service, the Festival of Nine Lessons and Carols, is broadcast live on BBC radio and television and is viewed or heard by more than 40 million people worldwide.

Christmas Eve are always crowded. At King's College Chapel, Cambridge, the beautiful Festival of Nine Lessons and Carols is celebrated on Christmas Eve afternoon. The chapel—begun by Henry VI in 1446 and completed by Henry VIII in 1515—is illuminated only by the flickering light of candles. The choir enters in procession, each singer carrying a lighted candle. During the service, readings from scripture alternate with the singing of traditional carols. Each year, there is also a newly commissioned carol. Nine Lessons and Carols services are also held on Christmas Eve at Westminster Abbey and other churches.

Carols old and new

In Greek and Roman days, a carol was a ring dance, an important part of all festivals. Words were added later, and eventually carols came to be associated only with the celebration of Christmas. "The Holly and the Ivy" and the Wassail song probably date back to the Middle Ages. "The Boar's Head Carol" and "Yule Log Carol," too, have been sung since ancient times in England.

Britain today has a host of favorite carols, including "The Twelve Days of Christmas," "Hark! The Herald Angels Sing," "Good King Wenceslas," "God Rest You Merry, Gentlemen," and "I Saw Three Ships Come Sailing In." "Once in Royal David's City" is sung at the start of the Festival of Nine Lessons and Carols at Cambridge. The words were written by Cecil Frances Alexander, wife of the Bishop of Derry. She wrote hundreds of hymns, and this one was composed for her godchildren, to tell them the story of Jesus's birth in simple verse. A popular carol of Victorian days, still occasionally sung today, is "In the Bleak Mid-Winter," the lyrics written by the famous English poet Christina Rosetti.

Like folk tales, carols are passed down from generation to generation. Few were printed until the 1800's, though a collection called a *Sette of Carols* was published about 1521. Carols were severely discouraged during the Puritan period in England, and they almost disappeared for some years. Only the long memories of country folk preserved them.

Welsh carols

The Welsh are a nation of singers and poets, holding national song and literary competitions called eisteddfods. The largest of these is held in August and draws enormous crowds every year. At

Christmas time, others are held just for caroling. Townsfolk gather in the market place, where trained choirs lead them in singing. New carols are composed each year for the Yuletide contests, and the winning songs are added to the repertoire of Christmas music.

Music is an integral part of Welsh life, especially at Christmas. The Welsh poet Dylan Thomas, in his essay "A Child's Christmas in Wales," wrote: "Always on Christmas night there was music. . . . Looking through my bedroom window, out into the moonlight and the unending smoke-colored snow, I could see the lights in the windows of all the other houses on our hill and hear the music rising from them up the long, steadily falling night. . . ."

Plygain ("before cock-crow"), the Christmas dawn service, was once held everywhere in Wales. Families would gather at the local village church in the dark hours of Christmas morning and sing, mainly unaccompanied, for hours. The overflowing church would be ablaze with candles as the singers caroled forth in solos, duets, trios, and full choruses, each group being careful not to repeat a carol that had already been sung. The words of the carols—all in Welsh—were handed down through the generations. According to one account from the 1800's, the rector might also include a sermon, but he made sure to keep it short, because the congregation became restless between carols! The tradition of plygain is still practiced in parts of central Wales, where the singing goes on from 3 a.m. to 6 a.m.

Schoolchildren participate in a Christingle service at Westminster Abbey in London. The Christingle, or "light of Christ," is an orange tied with a red ribbon and containing a candle and four sticks with fruits and nuts. This "lantern," a 200-year-old Welsh tradition, symbolizes the love of God for the world; the blood of Christ; the four seasons; and the fruits of the earth.

"The Ringing Isle"

Britain is sometimes called "The Ringing Isle," and the ancient art of *campanology* (bell-ringing) is still widely practiced. In early times, bells were considered almost human. They were given the names of saints and baptized. Sometimes, too, bells were named after their donors. St. Paul's Cathedral has its "Great Paul," Oxford is the home of "Great Tom," and of course the Houses of Parliament have "Big Ben."

At Christmas, bells throughout the land ring out the complicated sequences, called changes, over country fields and city rooftops. On Christmas Day morning in London, the bells of Westminster Abbey ring out with a clamoring peal as the Christmas service ends. At Crowland, in Lincolnshire, the choir once sang carols from the ancient battlements of Croyland Abbey on Christmas Eve. When the carols ended, bell ringers took over, sending out their own Christmas message.

Today, the choir no longer performs on the battlements, but the bells are rung on Christmas Day morning. Although the abbey lies in ruins, the north aisle of the old abbey chapel survives and has

The famous bells of Croyland are rung each Christmas Day morning. The north aisle of the old chapel is all that remains of Croyland Abbey, one of the most important monasteries in England before the Reformation.

become the village church. The bells of Croyland are unusual in that they have some of the longest pulls in England. Such a length is necessary because the bells are rung from the floor of the church rather than from up in the belfry.

Handbell ringers tour villages in many parishes during the weeks before Christmas, playing their traditional music as they go. The handbells of Standon, Hertfordshire, have belonged to the village since 1870.

The Devil's Knell

A custom called "Tolling the Devil's Knell" has been practiced for 700 years at Dewsbury, in Yorkshire. On Christmas Eve, bell ringers toll "Black Tom," the tenor bell of the parish church. Legend has it that Thomas de Soothill gave the bell to the church as a

token of remorse for having murdered a servant. He declared that it must sound a *knell* (announcement of death) every Christmas from that time forward. The ceremony proclaims an old belief that the Devil died at the birth of Christ. One ring is tolled for every year since Jesus was born, the final ring timed to strike exactly at midnight.

The joyful sounds of British Christmas have never been described more aptly than in a passage from Dickens's *Christmas Carol.* The newly reformed Scrooge has awakened on Christmas morning, "merry as a schoolboy" at having been given a second chance for happiness:

"He was checked in his transports by the churches ringing out the lustiest peals he had ever heard. Clash, clang, hammer; ding, dong, bell. Bell, dong, ding; hammer, clang, clash! Oh, glorious, glorious!

"Running to the window, he opened it, and put out his head. No fog, no mist; clear, bright, jovial, stirring, cold; cold, piping for the blood to dance to; Golden sunlight; Heavenly sky; sweet fresh air; merry bells. Oh, glorious. Glorious! Christmas Day!"

Bell ringers in a Somerset church prepare to let the bells peal forth on Christmas Day, as they do in churches throughout all of Britain.

Christmas Recipes

Angels on horseback

12 to 16 medium oysters
freshly ground pepper
12 to 16 thin slices bacon,
  partially cooked

3 to 4 slices toasted bread,
  quartered
lemon slices, halved
parsley sprigs

1. Remove oysters from shells. (Use only tightly closed oysters; discard half-opened ones.)
2. Season oysters with pepper and wrap a slice of bacon around each; if necessary, secure with a wooden pick or skewer.
3. Arrange on rack of a broiler pan.
4. Place under broiler about 4 inches from heat. Broil 7 to 8 minutes, turning several times until oysters are just done and bacon is browned evenly.
5. Put bacon-wrapped oysters on toast squares and arrange on a serving plate. Garnish with lemon half-slices and parsley.

Yield: 12 to 16 appetizers

Apple Yule logs

8 large cooking apples,
  pared and cored
1 cup soft breadcrumbs
½ cup finely chopped
  seeded raisins

¼ cup packed brown sugar
1 to 2 Tbsps. Scotch whisky
¼ cup light corn syrup
¼ cup dark corn syrup
½ cup Scotch whisky

1. Arrange apples in two rows in a large baking dish.
2. Mix breadcrumbs, raisins, brown sugar, and a little whisky to moisten. Spoon into apple centers. Mix corn syrups. Pour over stuffed apples.
3. Bake 30 to 40 minutes at 325 °F, or until apples are tender, basting frequently.
4. Pour syrup from dish into a small bowl.
5. Just before serving, warm the whisky, pour over the apples, and ignite. Serve apples with the sauce.
Note: If desired, chill the apples before flaming.

Yield: 8 servings

Roast potatoes

½ cup butter or margarine
8 large baking potatoes (about 4 pounds)
1 Tbsp. seasoned salt
½ cup chicken broth

1. Melt butter in a 13-x 9-inch baking pan.
2. Pare potatoes; roll in melted butter to coat well. Sprinkle with seasoned salt.
3. Bake 1 hour at 350 °F.
4. Turn potatoes and add chicken broth. Bake 30 to 45 minutes longer, turning occasionally.

Yield: 8 servings

Stuffed roast goose

1 roasting goose, 10 to 12 pounds
salt
½ cup butter
1 small bunch celery with leaves, finely chopped
1 small onion, finely chopped

4 cups soft breadcrumbs
1 tsp. mixed herbs
1 tsp. salt
¼ tsp. pepper
½ cup chicken stock

1. Remove neck and giblets; reserve liver. Discard fat. Rinse and dry goose. Rub skin with salt, then prick with a fork.
2. Heat butter in a skillet. Add goose liver and cook 5 minutes, turning occasionally. Remove from skillet. Add celery and onion to skillet; cook 5 minutes.
3. Chop liver and add to breadcrumbs along with cooked celery and onion, herbs, salt, and pepper. Add desired amount of stock and toss to mix.
4. Stuff goose with breadcrumb mixture; secure with skewers and cord. Put goose on rack in a shallow roasting pan.
5. Roast in a 325 °F oven 3 ½ to 4 hours, or until done; remove fat from pan occasionally.

Yield: 8 to 10 servings

Trifle

Sponge cake:

½ cup sifted cake flour
½ tsp. baking powder
⅛ tsp. salt
2 eggs
½ cup sugar
1 to 1 ½ tsps. lemon juice

3 Tbsps. hot milk
½ cup raspberry jam
½ cup slivered or sliced
   blanched almonds
1 cup sherry

Custard:

2 eggs
1 egg yolk
⅓ cup sugar
⅛ tsp. salt
1 ½ cups milk
1 ½ tsps. vanilla extract

Topping:

1 egg white
3 Tbsps. sugar
1 cup whipping cream,
  whipped
2 Tbsps. sherry
candied fruit for decorating

1. For cake, sift flour, baking powder, and salt together. Set aside.
2. Beat eggs until thick. Add sugar gradually while beating until thick. Mix in lemon juice. Sprinkle dry ingredients over egg mixture about one-fourth at a time; gently fold in until blended after each addition. Add hot milk all at one time and quickly mix just until smooth.
3. Turn batter into a greased (bottom only) 9-inch round layer cake pan.
4. Bake 15 to 25 minutes at 375 °F, or until cake tests done.
5. Cool about 10 minutes in pan on a wire rack. Remove from pan and cool completely.
6. Split cake layer and spread raspberry jam between layers. Cut into pieces and put into a glass serving bowl. Sprinkle with almonds. Pour sherry over all. Set aside 30 minutes.
7. Meanwhile, for custard, mix eggs, egg yolk, sugar, and salt in top of a double boiler. Add milk and stir over boiling water about 10 minutes, or until mixture coats a spoon. Stir in vanilla extract. Cool slightly.
8. Pour warm custard over cake in serving bowl. Allow to cool.
9. For topping, beat egg white until frothy. Add sugar gradually, beating thoroughly after each addition. Continue to beat until stiff peaks form.
10. Spread egg white over whipped cream and gently fold together. Fold in sherry. Spoon over custard layer. Decorate with candied fruit. Chill.

Yield: 8 to 10 servings

Fruitcake

4 cups all-purpose flour
2 tsps. baking powder
3 ¼ cups dried currants (1 pound)
2 ¾ cups golden raisins (1 pound)
2 cups diced mixed candied fruit (12 ounces)
1 ⅓ cups candied pineapple chunks (8 ounces)
1 cup halved red and green
   candied cherries (8 ounces)

1 cup chopped blanched
almonds
2 cups butter
2 cups sugar
8 eggs
½ cup brandy or rum

1. Sift flour and baking powder into a large bowl. Mix in fruit and nuts.
2. Cream butter and sugar. Add eggs, one at a time, beating well after each addition. Mix in fruit and nut mixture, then brandy.
3. Spoon batter into a thoroughly greased 10-x 3-inch springform pan.
4. Bake 2 ½ hours at 300 °F, or until cake tests done.
5. Cool cake 30 minutes in pan on a rack. Remove from pan and cool completely.

Yield: One 7-pound fruitcake

English gingered brandy snaps

¼ cup butter or margarine
¼ cup sugar
2 Tbsps. light corn syrup
1 tsp. molasses
½ cup all-purpose flour
½ tsp. ground ginger
⅛ tsp. ground nutmeg
1 Tbsp. brandy

Filling:
1 cup whipping
   cream, whipped
1 Tbsp. sugar
1 Tbsp. brandy

1. Combine butter, sugar, corn syrup, and molasses in a medium saucepan. Heat mixture over medium heat until butter is melted.
2. Mix flour, ginger, and nutmeg in a small bowl, then stir into the butter mixture. Stir in brandy.
3. Drop tablespoonfuls of the mixture 6 inches apart on greased cookie sheets.
4. Bake at 350 °F 8 to 10 minutes. Let cool for 30 seconds. Ease cookies off the cookie sheet with a spatula; then immediately roll loosely around a 6-inch tapered metal tube with the upper surface of each brandy snap on the outside. Cool on wire racks.
5. For filling, whip cream, add sugar and brandy, and mix well shortly before serving. Using a pastry bag fitted with a star tip, fill the cavity in the rolled brandy snap from each end.

Yield: 12 cookies

Butter shortbread

2 cups sifted all-purpose flour
6 Tbsps. sugar
2 Tbsps. cornstarch
¾ cup butter

1. Sift flour, sugar, and cornstarch into a bowl. Cut in butter until mixture becomes a soft dough (requires working beyond the stage when particles are the size of rice kernels).
2. Shape dough into a ball; knead lightly with fingertips until mixture holds together.
3. Press into a buttered 8- or 9-inch round layer cake pan. Flute the edge. Prick dough thoroughly with a fork.
4. Bake 35 to 40 minutes at 350 °F, or until lightly browned. Remove from oven when almost done. Mark into sections with a knife. Return to oven until baked.
5. Cool in pan.

Yield: 8 to 10 pieces

Dickens's wassail bowl

3 baking apples, cored and 1-inch strip pared from stem end
¼ cup sugar
1 cup water
4 quarts ale
2 Tbsps. each ground cinnamon, ginger, and nutmeg
1 quart sherry
1 ½ cups sugar
2 lemons, peeled (cut in 2-inch pieces) and juiced
toast triangles

1. Put apples into a deep casserole.
2. Combine ¼ cup sugar and the water in a saucepan; bring to a boil. Pour syrup over apples. Cover casserole.
3. Bake at 350 °F 30 to 40 minutes, or until apples are tender, basting occasionally.
4. Pour ale into a saucepan and heat on low heat until it foams. Add spices, sherry, 1 ½ cups sugar, lemon peel, and lemon juice. Heat, stirring until sugar is dissolved. Set aside 20 minutes.
5. Reheat mixture and pour through a double thickness of cheesecloth into a heatproof punch bowl. Add apples.
6. Ladle wassail into cups; garnish with lemon peel. Serve with toast triangles.

Yield: About 5 quarts

Christmas Crafts

Stained Glass Snowflake

1. Fold a sheet of white paper in half (a).
   Then fold it in half again (b).

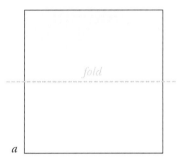

2. Use a pencil and ruler to lightly draw a diagonal line from one corner to the other. Bring the bottom edge of the paper up to the diagonal line and fold (c).

   Next, bring the left edge of the paper down to the diagonal line and fold (d).

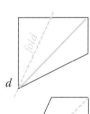

   Then fold along the diagonal line (e). You should now have a triangular shape.

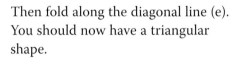

3. Trace the pattern (right) onto the folded paper, placing the pattern on the triangle exactly as shown. Cut away the areas shaded in blue. Unfold the paper to reveal a snowflake.

4. Cut out small squares from the colored tissue paper. Glue these squares over the holes on one side of the snowflake. (The side with the glued squares is the backside.)

5. Cut out a second snowflake following steps 1 thru 3. Glue it to the backside of the first snowflake. You may need to trim some edges that do not quite match up.

6. Using the needle and thread, sew a loop into the snowflake.

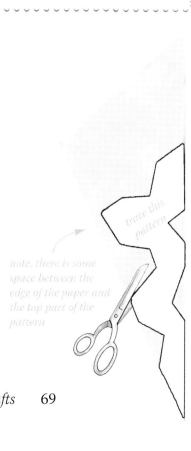

trace this pattern

note, there is some space between the edge of the paper and the top part of the pattern

Welsh border fan

1. Tie three straws together with the thread and gently spread them apart. We'll call the straws *a*, *b*, and *c*, from right to left.

2. Insert a new straw *d* under *a* and over *b*. Insert another new straw *e* under *c* and over *d*.

3. Gently bend *a* back, slip it under *b* and over *e*, and let it lie to the left. Repeat the same with *c*, placing it under *d* and over *a* and letting it lie to the right.

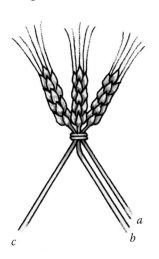

4. Repeat with outside right-hand straw *b* and outside left-hand straw *d*.

5. Insert another new straw under the outside right-hand straw *e* and over all other straws and let it lie to the left. Lock this into position by taking *e* and repeating step 3, making sure that it passes under *c* and over *d*.

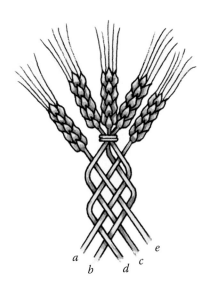

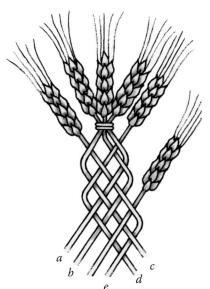

6. Continue working from right to left, until you've used 17 straws. Note that as the work progresses the outside straw travels over an increasing number of other straws.

7. To finish off fan, tie the ends of the straws of each group together with thread and trim off at an angle.

8. Tie the remaining four straws together, holding 2 facing one way and 2 facing the other. Fold the straws gently in half and connect to other straws as shown. Ribbons may be used to join here if desired.

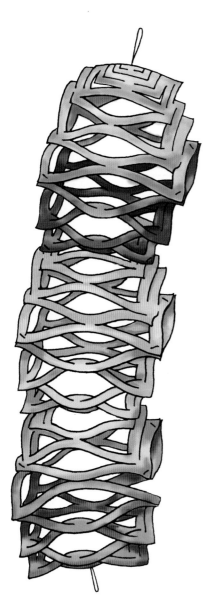

Concertina

1. Cut a 7-inch square from construction paper or other similarly sturdy paper. Fold the square in half to form a rectangle. Fold this in half again, forming a small square. Then fold the small square diagonally to form a triangle.

2. With sharp scissors, make a series of cuts, alternating from side to side. Each cut should end within ⅛ inch of the opposite edge. The first cut should be made about ½ inch in from the side and should begin on the folded edge of the triangle. The remaining cuts should be about ⅜-inch apart.

3. After making all cuts, unfold the paper to its original size and straighten out creases by bending in the opposite direction.

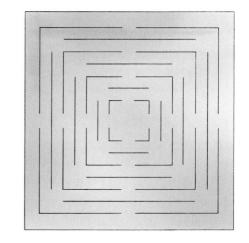

4. Repeat the above steps, alternating between colored squares of paper if desired, the number depending on how long you want the finished chain to be. Make sure all squares are the same size.

Materials
- several sheets of construction paper of various colors or all of the same color
- scissors
- stapler

5. Staple the finished squares together: Join squares *a* and *b* by stapling outer corners to outer corners; join squares *b* and *c* by stapling their inner corners together. Then staple the outer corners of *c* to *d* and repeat for the remaining squares.

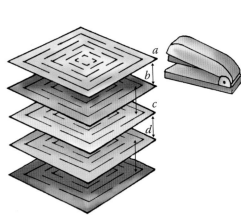

6. Stretch the chain and hang across a wall or from a ceiling.

Christmas Carols

Away in a Manger

Anonymous

J. R. Murray, 1877 [WE]

1. A - way in a man - ger, no crib for a bed, The lit - tle Lord
2. The cat - tle are low - ing, the Ba - by a - wakes, But lit - tle Lord
3. Be near me, Lord Je - sus, I ask Thee to stay Close by me for -

Je - sus laid down His sweet head. The stars in the sky____looked
Je - sus, no cry - ing He makes. I love Thee, Lord Je - sus, look
ev - er, and love me, I pray. Bless all the dear chil - dren in

down where He lay, The lit - tle Lord Je sus, a - sleep on the hay.
down from the sky, And stay by my cra - dle till morn - ing is nigh,
Thy ten - der care, And fit us for Heav - en to live with Thee there.

Coventry Carol

Robert Croo, 1543

English Melody, 1591

Andante sostenuto

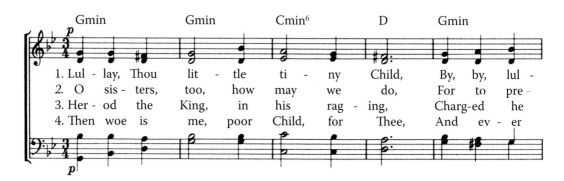

1. Lul - lay, Thou lit - tle ti - ny Child, By, by, lul -
2. O sis - ters, too, how may we do, For to pre -
3. Her - od the King, in his rag - ing, Charg-ed he
4. Then woe is me, poor Child, for Thee, And ev - er

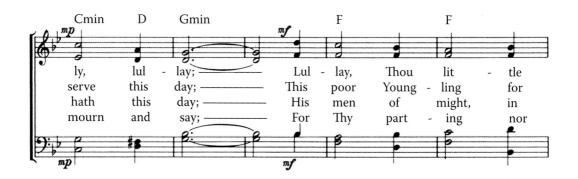

ly, lul - lay; Lul - lay, Thou lit - tle
serve this day; This poor Young - ling for
hath this day; His men of might, in
mourn and say; For Thy part - ing nor

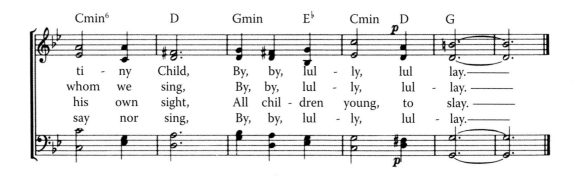

ti - ny Child, By, by, lul - ly, lul lay.
whom we sing, By, by, lul - ly, lul - lay.
his own sight, All chil - dren young, to slay.
say nor sing, By, by, lul - ly, lul - lay.

Deck the Hall with Boughs of Holly

Traditional Welsh

Old Welsh Carol

1. Deck the hall with boughs of hol - ly,
2. See the blaz - ing Yule be - fore us,
3. Fast a - way the old year pass - es,
Fa la la la la, la la la la,

'Tis the sea - son to be jol - ly,
Strike the harp and join the cho - rus,
Hail the new, ye lads and lass - es,
Fa la la la la, la la la la.

Don we now our gay ap - par - rel,
Fol - low me in mer - ry meas - ure,
Sing we joy - ous all to - geth - er,
Fa__ la la__ la la la la,

Troll the an cient Yule - tide car - ol,
While I tell of Yule - tide treas - ure,
Heed -less of the wind and weath -er,
Fa la la la la la la la la.

On Christmas Night (Sussex Carol)

Traditional English, alt. [GKE]   Traditional English [WE]

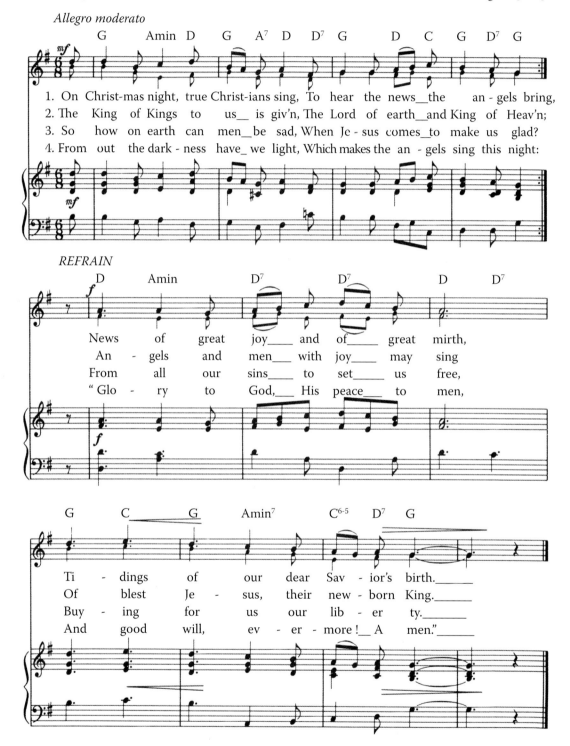

The Boar's Head Carol

17th Century English

18th Century English Carol [WE]

1. The boar's head in hand bear I, Be - decked with bays and rose-ma -ry; And I
2. The boar's head as I un - der-stand is the fin - est dish in all the land, When
3. Our stew-ard hath pro - vid - ed this In honor of the King of Bliss, Which

pray you, my mas-ters, be mer - ry, Quot es - tis in con - vi - vi - o,[1]
thus be - decked with a gay gar - land, Let us ser - vi - re can - ti - co.[2]
on this day to be serv-ed is, In Re - gi - nen- si a - tri - o.[3]

REFRAIN

Ca - put a pri de - fe - ro, Red - dens lau- des Do - mi - no.[4]

[1]You who are at this feast
[2]Serve by singing
[3]In the royal hall

[4]The boar's head I bear,
Giving praises to the Lord.

We Wish You a Merry Christmas

Traditional English

Traditional English [WE]

When Christ Was Born of Mary Free

Harleian Manuscript, 1456

16th Century English [WE]

Acknowledgments

The publishers gratefully acknowledge the following sources for photography. All illustrations and maps were prepared by WORLD BOOK unless otherwise noted.

Cover: © hammondovi/iStockphoto

2-3: © Sean Gladwell, Alamy Images

5: © stocker1970/Shutterstock

6: © Travel Pictures/SuperStock

8: © Prisma/SuperStock; © Rex USA

9: © WH CHOW/Shutterstock

10: © Andy Rain, epa/Corbis; © Britain on View/Getty Images

11: © AWL Images/Masterfile

12: © AWL Images/Masterfile

13: © Mary Evans Picture Library; © Echo/Getty Images

14: © Toby Melville, Reuters

15: © Simone Becchetti, iStockphoto; © Paul Viant, Getty Images

16: © Colin Underhill, Alamy Images

18: Illustration by Pauline Baynes (© Williams College Oxford Programme/Mary Evans Picture Library)

19: © Illustrated London News/Mary Evans Picture Library

20: Illustration by Pauline Baynes (© Williams College Oxford Programme/Mary Evans Picture Library)

21: © Lebrecht Music and Arts Photo Library/Alamy Images; © Mary Evans Picture Library

22: Illustration by Pauline Baynes (© Williams College Oxford Programme/Mary Evans Picture Library)

23: © Classic Image/Alamy Images

24: © iStockphoto/Thinkstock

25: © ARPL/HIP/The Image Works; © Medici/Mary Evans Picture Library

26: © NHPA/SuperStock; © Bettmann/Corbis/AP Images

27: Illustration by Pauline Baynes (© Williams College Oxford Programme/Mary Evans Picture Library)

28-35: Kinuko Craft

36: © Art Directors & TRIP/Alamy Images

38: © Liam Norris, Cultura/Getty Images; © image100/SuperStock

39: © Kumar Sriskandan, Alamy Images

40: © Art Directors & TRIP/Alamy Images

41: © Express Newspapers/AP Images

42-43: © Daniel Berehulak, Getty Images

44: © Geoff Caddick, PA/AP Images

45: © Adrian Sherratt/Alamy Images

46: © Geoff Moore, Rex USA

47: © Veryan Dale, Alamy Images

48: © Homer Sykes, CountrySideCollection/Alamy Images

50: © Homer Sykes, CountrySideCollection/Alamy Images

52: © Jeff Morgan 16/Alamy Images

53: © Stephen Spraggon, Alamy Images; © Christopher Furlong, Getty Images; © Tristan Tan, Shutterstock

54: Jeremy Carter-Gordon

55: © Danny Lawson, PA/AP Images

56: © Matthew Lloyd, Getty Images

57: © UK History/Alamy Images

58: © Geoffrey Robinson, Alamy Images

61: © Alex Segre, Alamy Images

62: © Dave Porter, Alamy Images

63: © Stephen Parker, Alamy Images

64: © Monkey Business Images/Shutterstock

65: © Photocrea/Shutterstock

66: © abimages/Shutterstock

67: © Thinkstock

68: © Shutterstock

Craft illustrations:
Mel Klapholz/Brenda Tropinski

Advent calendar:
© The Art Gallery Collection/Alamy Images

Advent calendar and recipe card illustrations:
Eileen Mueller Neill

Recipe consultant and recipe card editor:
Karen Zack Ingebretsen